OFF-ROAD CARS

BY ASHLEY GISH

T0016454

CREATIVE EDUCATION • CREATIVE PAPERBACKS

Published by Creative Education and Creative Paperbacks
P.O. Box 227, Mankato, Minnesota 56002
Creative Education and Creative Paperbacks are imprints of
The Creative Company
www.thecreativecompany.us

Design by The Design Lab
Production by Joe Kahnke
Art direction by Rita Marshall
Printed in China

Photographs by A Girls Guide to Cars (TOTAL CHAOS Fabrication),
Alamy (Juan Aunion, Mike Ingalsbee/Southcreek Global/ZUMA-
press.com, S. Parente - Best of Travel – RM), Dreamstime (Lukas
Gojda, Vladimir Melnik), Getty Images (Bob D'Olivo/The Enthusiast
Network), iStockphoto (wbgorex, wdalton), Shutterstock (cristiano
barni, Zsolt Biczo, Rodrigo Garrido, muph, Arnon Polin, Vdant85,
Christian Vinces)

Library of Congress Cataloging-in-Publication Data
Names: Gish, Ashley, author.
Title: Off-road cars / Ashley Gish.
Series: Amazing racing cars.
Includes bibliographical references and index.
Summary: A fast-paced, high-interest introduction to off-road cars,
rugged vehicles known for their wide, tough tires and use in off-road
races. Also included is a biographical story about off-road driver
Emily Miller.
Identifiers: LCCN: 2019049659
ISBN 978-1-64026-289-8 (hardcover)
ISBN 978-1-62832-821-9 (pbk)
ISBN 978-1-64000-419-1 (eBook)
Subjects: LCSH: Off-road vehicles—Juvenile literature.
Classification: LCC TL235.6.G57 2021 / DDC 629.228/8—dc23

CCSS: RI.1.1, 2, 4, 5, 6, 7; RI.2.2, 5, 6, 7, 10; RI.3.1, 5, 7, 8;
RF.1.1, 3, 4; RF.2.3, 4

First Edition HC 9 8 7 6 5 4 3 2 1
First Edition PBK 9 8 7 6 5 4 3 2 1

Table of Contents

Ed Pearlman and Don Francisco started the National Off-Road Racing Association (NORRA) in California. NORRA hosted the first official off-road event in 1967. It was called the Mexican 1000 Rally.

The Mexican 1000 sends drivers 1,000 miles (1,609 km) through the desert in Baja, Mexico.

A co-driver reads the map and tells the driver about upcoming problems.

Today, there are many kinds of off-road vehicles. Some are built for races. Others are used by the military. Off-road vehicles are fitted with wide, tough tires. They drive over rough **terrain**.

terrain an area of land, often with unique features

Groups like SCORE International and the Mud Racers Association organize races. Two popular off-road events are desert racing and mudding.

To drive through mud, off-road cars need large tires with deep grooves.

Most desert races run from 25 to 1,000 miles (40.2–1,609 km). Baja Bugs race along desert courses. Dune buggies are popular in desert races, too.

Vehicles on sand dunes might sink or slide backwards.

In sand races, vehicles have tall flags that mark the car's location above the dust.

Dune buggies do not look like regular cars. Some do not have side doors. Drivers have to slide down into the seat from the roof. Most dune buggies have lightweight bodies made of **fiberglass**.

fiberglass strong material made from a mixture of glass and plastic fibers

Mud races are shorter than desert races. The goal in these races is to get as far through a mud pit as possible. Wide tires with knobby bumps help vehicles roll through deep mud. Sometimes vehicles get stuck. If two or more vehicles make it through the mud pit, the fastest wins.

Off-road vehicles come in a variety of shapes and sizes.

*Shifting sands can make
driving down a sand dune
as difficult as climbing it.*

Off-road vehicles are separated into classes. Each class has its own rules. Racing vehicles in limited classes must have **stock** parts. But unlimited classes can use **aftermarket** parts.

aftermarket describing parts that are bought to replace existing parts

stock describing parts that come with the vehicle from the factory

Good suspension helps keep tires on the road and offers a smoother ride.

An off-road vehicle's **suspension** is important. Speeding over a bump can send the vehicle flying through the air. A good suspension gives drivers better control on rough terrain.

suspension the system of springs and shock absorbers that gives a vehicle stability

Off-road racing is an exciting sport. It is fun to watch these amazing vehicles plow through mud, float over sand dunes, and climb up hills.

Long races are divided into sections, called stages, with breaks between each part.

Emily Miller was 30 years old when she raced for the first time. She fell in love with the sport. Before long, Emily tried off-road racing. She enjoyed getting her boots dirty and thought other women would, too. She founded Rebelle Rally in 2016. Drivers can use only maps to find their way through areas of Nevada and California—no phones allowed. Emily encourages girls and women to push past their comfort zones and live confidently.

Read More

Abdo, Kenny. *Dune Buggies*. Minneapolis: Abdo Zoom, 2018.

Chandler, Matt. *The Tech Behind Off-Road Vehicles*. North Mankato, Minn.: Capstone Press, 2020.

Shaffer, Lindsay. *4x4 Trucks*. Minneapolis: Bellwether Media, 2019.

Websites

Kiddle: Off-Road Vehicle Facts for Kids
https://kids.kiddle.co/Off-road_vehicle
See pictures of off-road vehicles, and read more about these rugged machines.

Mojave Desert
https://biomemojavedesert.weebly.com/
Learn about the Mojave Desert, a popular place to go off-roading.

YouTube: Lucas Oil Off Road
https://www.youtube.com/user/lucasoiloffroad
Watch videos of short-course off-road races and interviews with drivers.

Note: Every effort has been made to ensure that the websites listed above are suitable for children, that they have educational value, and that they contain no inappropriate material. However, because of the nature of the Internet, it is impossible to guarantee that these sites will remain active indefinitely or that their contents will not be altered.

Index